This is a work of fiction. References to real people, events, establishments, organizations, or locales are intended only to provide a sense of authenticity and are used fictitiously. All other characters, and all incidents and dialogue are drawn from the author's imagination and are not to be construed as real.

I WANT THE TRUTH. Copyright © 2023 Andrea Martinez. All rights reserved. Printed in the United States of America. For information, address Acorn Publishing, LLC, 3943 Irvine Blvd. Ste. 218, Irvine, CA 92602

www.acornpublishingllc.com

Interior designed by Kat Ross
Cover design by Damonza

Anti-Piracy Warning: The unauthorized reproduction or distribution of a copyrighted work is illegal. Criminal copyright infringement, including infringement without monetary gain, is investigated by the FBI and is punishable by up to five years in federal prison and a fine of $250,000.

All rights reserved. No part of this book may be used or reproduced in any manner whatsoever, including Internet usage, without written permission from the author.

ISBN-13: 979-8-88528-058-7 (hardcover)

ISBN-13: 979-8-88528-057-0 (paperback)

Library of Congress Control Number: 2023914879

I WANT THE TRUTH

ANDREA MARTINEZ

FROM THE TINY ACORN...
GROWS THE MIGHTY OAK

This book is dedicated to God Himself. His hand and His words guided me through the writing of this book. I can't thank Him enough for loving me and for not leaving me in the mess that I unknowingly, and at times knowingly, caused myself.

I also cannot thank Him sufficiently for my three blessings. My babies. They mean everything to me, and it was them and their words that God used to help me to never give up. Especially my Vic. He was the one who never left mama's side and he taught his mama about love, sacrifice and faith!

INTRODUCTION

Love. We all have different thoughts about it. Some of us long for it, countless others run from it, a great many of us have given up on it — and then there are those of us who are just completely over it. Well, whichever category you fit into, one question remains. Do we even really know what this word *"love"* means?

I must admit, I thought I did. And now I know that I was completely unaware of the true meaning of *"love."* And knowing what I know now, there is just no way possible I would have ever figured it out in this lifetime had I stayed on the path I walked.

In this book, I am going to walk you through everything I've learned about *love*, and I am going to be completely transparent. My hope is that you will learn from my mistakes and my pain. I took a journey I would not wish on anyone, but I would do it all again for the simple fact that the outcome was INCREDIBLE!

I pray that this book will help others in such a way that they can use my pain to forfeit even just a bit of their own. I do not wish this pain on anyone, but what we do not realize is that living in our ignorance about *love* can bring so much more pain and heartache than we would go through in the waiting process.

As you read, I want you to remember that I am just an ordinary person like anyone else. I am not a pastor or a speaker or anything other than a regular woman, who was sick and tired of going through the same pain over and over again. I became so full of pain, I begged God to reveal to me what the issue was and why so many of us are dealing with it. Boy, did He show me, and He did so because I promised to tell all of you, as well.

Let's dive into this journey together and remember, if you are reading this and at any time begin to feel like it does not pertain to you because you are a mess and no one knows the horrible things you have done or the person you really are, then you OBVIOUSLY don't know me! I am the biggest hot mess around.

If God can come through for me, despite all of my sin, mistakes, bad choices and crazy decision-making, then He can surely come through for anyone. Trust me when I say that He longs to come through for you, but He's anxiously waiting for you to ask Him.

Matthew 7:7-11. *"Ask and it shall be given you, seek and ye shall find, knock and the door will be open unto you."*

Chapter One

WHAT IS REAL LOVE? DO WE REALLY KNOW?

*D*o any of us really even know the real meaning of what our hearts desire the most in our lives? Isn't that a scary thought? We all desire *love* and to be loved for exactly who we are (and trust me, we all desire this even if your feelings say otherwise, that is why God puts so much emphasis on it in His Word.) and yet even with this strong desire in the core of our being, we have no real idea what it is that we are really longing for. Let's chew on that for a bit. How can we want something so badly and even feel it so strongly yet be so misled or uneducated about what it is we all really long for? Real *Love*.

So the first thing I had to ask myself when I was thinking about *love* and the type of *love* I wanted in my life was, "What was I basing my desire on and did I even know what *Love* really was?" I actually never thought about this question much at all. It was not until I had been hurt too many times to count, and in so many different ways, I finally asked God, "What the heck is the problem with these men you made? I mean, you want us to have Godly marriages but with who? Are there special people you have hidden, and you only send them down when someone is almost perfect or what?"

Oh, and men, I am sure there are some of you who feel the

same way about us. Not all of us are looking for money, a sugar daddy, or just a fling. Sadly, it is just as difficult for you, as well.

I know this may sound odd, but this is exactly where I was in my journey and it was exactly how I felt. I longed for someone to *love* me just for me for many years, and it seemed as though the loving partnership I sought was just not in the cards for me. It finally occurred to me that I was not the only one who felt this way. A great many people feel the same way and, if that's the case, then what is the problem?

First, I think the problem begins with our perception of what real *love* is. Most women have this Hallmark ideal, which is nothing more than pure fantasy. We all know those types of relationships do not exist. To be honest, I am glad they don't. Why? you might ask. Well, I have no desire to own a bakery and fall in *love* with the only hot guy in town, who finally decided to take time off from running the successful company he owns to come home for Christmas because his mother guilted him into it. No, thank you. I'm good.

And since we are on the topic of fantasy, men, you are no different than women. You all have major preconceived perceptions, as well. FYI: we have no desire to become Stepford wives (robots that do as you command), and most of us will never look like the women online that you have no business looking at anyhow. (Yes, I went there.)

So you see, we all have our perceptions of what *Love* is. Because most of them are incorrect, we never succeed in finding *love*. We end up settling or moving from one to the next and just being completely unhappy. Some of you may be reading this and saying to yourselves, *"Well, I do not have a perception like that and I know what love really is so this doesn't even pertain to me."* Or you might be thinking, *I don't even care that much about finding love, because I'm good all by myself and I have everything I need.*

I am so happy you are confident in yourself. That is a good thing, of course. But if you didn't long for *love*, why did you even decide to read this book to begin with? We must be honest with ourselves about the how and why of our feelings. Our emotions are usually deeply rooted in our pasts and the circumstances surrounding our pasts.

God will reveal our past wounds and heal us if we simply ask Him, which is exactly what He is waiting for us to do. He does not want us to feel hurt. Yet, He will never force anything upon us. He gave us free will. He is so respectful of us and what we want, He waits for us for as long as it takes until we finally seek His guidance.

It is then that God becomes excited and overjoyed, because now we have given Him permission to do what only He can do. We'd best believe He will do it. It is exactly what He has wanted to do for us since He made us. Will it be easy? Of course, not. Healing never is, but it will be much easier than looking for *love* over and over again and adding more heartbreak and pain to the hurts we've already carried for so many years.

We all long for *love* in some aspect of our lives. I know this because I faithfully read the Bible. This is why God focuses so much on *Love* in His Word.

You may ask yourself, what is the correct perception and how do we obtain it? Well, most of us know the verse 1 Corinthians 13: 4-8. We have heard these words a thousand times or more at church while growing up. We have seen them etched onto every cup and wall art piece at Hobby Lobby. Or, perhaps, you may never have even heard the words before.

Either way, I guarantee that most of us are in the same boat when it comes to really understanding the meaning of the verse and what God has to say about it. I am going to go through this passage with you just as God did with me when I asked Him about it. I hope you are ready for this because I wasn't. But why wait any longer? Let's just jump in head-first and do this thing already.

1 Corinthians 13:4-8 *"Love is patient and kind. Love is not jealous or boastful or proud or rude. It does not demand its own way. It is not irritable, and it keeps no record of being wronged. It does not rejoice*

about injustice but rejoices whenever the truth wins out. Love never gives up, never loses faith, is always hopeful, and endures through every circumstance. Prophecy and speaking in unknown languages and special knowledge will become useless. But Love will last forever."

There is so much to unpack in this tiny passage. Having read it a hundred times over, and even memorizing it in elementary school, nothing — and I mean nothing — could have prepared me for what I am about to show you. This was a complete struggle for me when God began to reveal so many things and peel back all of my misconceptions on this tiny little word that I held so close to my heart. This word was such a driving force in my life, yet I had no idea what I even desired.

I don't know about y'all, but I failed right out the gate. Patient and kind. I mean, I can be kind for the most part — sometimes — when I feel like it, but patient? Those who know me realize that patience is my Achilles heel. One of them, anyway. I was blessed with more heels than the norm and I'm not talking about Louboutins (shoes). I want things when I want them, and that usually translates to right now.

Oh, I can wait if I must, but my waiting usually goes like this. *"Okay, God, I promise I'll wait on you. I will do whatever you ask of me, and I will totally trust you and your timing."* A week later, I would likely say, *"God, I've been waiting forever now and to be honest, I'm over it. You said You were going to come through for me, and I haven't seen anything. What's going on? I have done everything you told me to do. I'm good now, so you can deliver on your promise at any time. Remember, I'm ready. In Jesus's Name."*

Yes, I know that sounds funny. Sad to say, it is my truth. I told you, patience is not my deal, and long-suffering wasn't a word in my vocabulary.

As I began to really read this passage and dissect it piece by piece, I was mortified. I knew all about patience in my mind, but did I really? I mean, how hard have I really studied on it? It was at that moment that I felt the urge to begin really looking at the word and what it really means to be patient. I began to look up definitions to this word, and I was mind-blown.

The first definition was as follows, *"Patience: The capacity to accept or tolerate delay, trouble, or suffering without getting angry or upset."* The second definition I found was, *"Patience: the bearing of provocation (the action or speech that makes someone annoyed or angry, especially deliberately) annoyance, misfortune, or pain without complaint, loss of temper, irritation, or the like."*

The preceding definitions require consideration and thought, but I urge you to consider the third and final one from Wikipedia. It seriously blew my mind. *"Patience: (or forbearance), which means self-control, restraint and tolerance, is the ability to endure (to suffer something painful or difficult, patiently) difficult circumstances. Patience may involve perseverance, i.e. the continued effort to do or achieve something despite difficulties, failure, or opposition, in the face of delay; tolerance of provocation without responding in disrespect/anger; or forbearance when under strain, especially when forced with longer-term difficulties, or being able to wait for a long amount of time without getting irritated or bored. Patience is the level of endurance, the fact or power of enduring an unpleasant or difficult process or situation without giving way, one can have before disrespect. It is also used to refer to the character trait of being steadfast, resolutely or dutifully firm and unwavering."*

Now, I don't know about you, but after reading all of this, I just knew this was an only God thing, because no living creature, not even animals, can walk in this type of character. I mean even dogs, as much as they love us, can still get snappy at times. When I think of all the characteristics listed and put it all into perspective, the ONLY one that comes to my mind is Jesus. I think of Him in all of the movies I have seen, and even though they were actors, the portrayals of Him were always real. Jesus was always very loving, kind and patient, which is exactly what draws you into the characters. Now if that can be done by actors, how much more do you think it can be done through the real one? Jesus.

I mean, who can even come close to one word of this verse, let alone the entire passage? It's as if God had set us up to fail on this one and that is exactly what we will do. Fail, over and over again, if we try to do it in our own strength. We must lean on God and His strength alone to even begin to understand the meaning of true *love*, let alone walking in it.

Does that mean we will never fail once we add God and His strength to the equation? Of course not, but the difference between doing it in our own strength as opposed to His is that when we do fail, and we will, we are now covered by His grace. He will continue to strengthen us so that we will become much better at it as opposed to failing miserably over and over again. We will always be working on it until the Father calls us home; however, we will keep getting better at it and it will be easier as we go.

If we look at what the true meaning of *love* is in 1 Corinthians 13, it is simply impossible to achieve. I concluded that that was exactly why we, as a people, had so many issues with *love*. It's impossible to give out something that we ourselves do not even possess. It was at this point that I remember taking this to God and asking Him what it was that I was missing. Did He really expect us to do all of this and, if so, how? I mean even with Him, as I stated above, it would still be extremely difficult.

As I continued to pray and ask for wisdom on this, He spoke to me so clearly and lovingly. He told me to look at every part of the passage and really study the meaning of each. I promised myself that I would be obedient in all that He asked of me, because I really was tired of being in the wilderness. I knew I had been just like the Israelites, and I'd wandered in this wilderness way longer than needed.

I wound up this way because of so many wrong choices I had made. I hadn't really wanted to take the time and do the work and to allow Him to heal me of all of my past, my incorrect thinking patterns, and even some of my core beliefs. It was much easier to apply band-aids to my wounds and to continue to fill my voids with all sorts of mess, to mask the pain.

The question God brought to mind was this: *Was I really successful at masking my pain, or was I just making things much worse for not only myself, but for my children and so many others in my life?* It was at this moment God reminded me that everything we do not only has an effect on us but on so many others, as well.

Let's look into this outlandish definition. I mean, really? Who has this type of character? I know a few really patient people, and they would even fail this one after reading all these definitions. *To accept/tolerate delay, trouble or suffering without getting angry or upset.* Is this even a thing? I mean, I know some people may not get as angry as I can at times, but not even being able to be upset? Geez.

Then it says, *bearing all hard things without complaint, loss of temper or irritation.* Are you kidding me? We are not even allowed to get irritated. And this does not mean just on the outside, y'all. It means on the inside too, because God knows our hearts and we cannot hide our feelings. O.M.G. Forget this word already. I'm already over it.

But wait, there's more. *Being able to wait for a long amount of time without getting irritated or bored.* This is what it meant to be steadfast. Ha, ha, ha! I'm so sorry, but this is just comical to me. Who made up this nonsense? We all might as well ask God to take us now, because it's over.

Why in the name of all things would God ask us to do something so impossible? As I stated above, was He just being mean and setting us up to fail miserably? Why? And not to mention the very first characteristic in the definition of *love*. Why even bother looking at the rest if this is the nonsense we are getting right out the gate? Talk about feeling discouraged. No wonder it is so hard to find *love*. No one can do it. Not even the first characteristic is attainable so just throw the whole word in the garbage, because it's over. Right? Wrong! We must continue because God has a plan. I promise you.

I can write an entire book on patience itself, but I'd rather not. I'm sure I will be called to do that later, just because I said, "I'd rather not." Anyhow, now we have an understanding of what true patience is and that there is no way we can ever achieve it (without God, of course) and even then, we still will not be able to perfect it. Let's move on to the next characteristic God revealed to me.

Next up is, *Love* is kind. That one is more understandable. When you really think about it, you should wonder, *are we always kind to others?* Especially in those times where they are not so kind to us.

For the most part, it is pretty easy to be kind to kind people. God says we are to be kind to everyone, no matter how they treat us. As I began to look up the word, I remember thinking to myself, everyone knows what this word means, maybe I can just skip over the definition of this one. Ha! God wasn't thrilled so this is what I found. *Kind or Kindness: The quality of being friendly, generous, and considerate.*

Well, as soon as I finished reading this definition, God hit me with this one. Why does it say "quality" and not "act"? I mean, most of us think of kindness as being an act. For example, *"That was a great act of kindness you showed today."* Right? This is what we are used to saying, but God went deeper (of course, He did) to show me that it really is not an act at all. Instead, it is a "quality" just as the definition describes.

Well, what does quality mean? The definition of quality: *The degree of excellence of something.* So, if you put it all in perspective, what being kind really means is that we obtain excellence (because God is never less than that) in how friendly, generous, and considerate we are towards others. Now this was all in just the second word of the definition of kindness. As I continued, I thought to myself, generous? How is that word defined in kindness? Isn't that a characteristic all on its own? Why mix it with kindness?

It was then that God revealed to me that you cannot be

stingy and kind at the same time. Now remember, this is a characteristic that is to be expected and exhibited to everyone, not just those we pick and choose. That stated, we are to be generous with everyone and, if not, then we are not truly showing kindness at all. That to me was crazy. I thought, Kindness. This an easy one. Just to be nice to everyone. Boy, was I wrong yet again.

Are we really being kind to everyone after all? I know I'm not, and I do know that God does not like things to be done halfway. He says a great deal about this in His Word. Revelation 3:16: *"But since you are like lukewarm water, neither hot nor cold, I will spit you out of my mouth!"* Not only are these letters in red in the Bible, but there is an exclamation point attached. So you know God means business on this one. Once again, another characteristic we cannot attain on our own but only through Him and His strength.

Another point that God showed me was that being generous is not always a financial action. Yes, it is part of it, but depending on the situation, that may be much easier to some than others. I mean, giving money to someone is generous. Yes, but so is giving of your time, or giving of yourself, and most of the time those things are much more difficult to give. At least, they are for me. It is a complete act of selflessness and boy, can we all use a bit more of that these days.

A great many of us are so busy and wrapped up in our own stressful lives, we barely have the time, if at all, to give to our families or ourselves, for that matter. So the notion of being generous with our time is just unrealistic. If there is one thing I have learned in my journey with God, it's that He never ever does anything in the way we think He should; it is usually the opposite of what we would do or something so out there, we would never even think of it to begin with. Just consider some of the ways in which Jesus handled stressful issues in the Bible.

The first situation that comes to my mind is the five loaves and two fish situation. I mean, come on. You have way over five thousand people, chillin' and hungry, and no food to feed this type of crowd — or any crowd for that matter. Who wouldn't freak out when Jesus says to feed them? Yet here comes a boy with his little lunch that his mama packed him and offered it to Jesus to help. This is exactly why Jesus tells us to come to Him as little children.

The faith that this little one had to think his lunch could help and the kindness that we so struggle to show to others, was just that easy for this little one. Without hesitation, he offered all he had to feed anyone he could. Wow, right? I mean, when I am hungry and have not eaten in a bit, don't even think about asking me for my food. I know the exact word to use in this situation. That word is selfish, and it sure does not show up in the definition of kindness. I even looked back a few times. Nope, not there.

What this shows me is that if we are called to be like Christ and *love* as He does then we are to pretty much do the opposite of what our flesh longs to do. Talk about tough, and yet, I guess if it was easy, we would all be doing it no problem and there would be no need for books like this one. Clearly, we have a lot to learn so let's just keep going and get thrashed together. Let me say it nicely. Let's get put in check together; it's less embarrassing that way. Ha, ha, ha.

Chapter Two
KEEPING IT 100

Let's move on from patience and kindness. I think I have had enough of that for one day. We are now faced with the next challenges in the aspect of *love*. *Love* is not jealous, boastful or proud or rude. Well, if for some reason you were able to talk yourself into thinking that you were pretty on point with being patient and kind to others, there is no way you are going to pass this section with flying colors.

Let's start with the obvious. *Love* is not jealous. Well, I don't know about you, but if a woman talks to my man and she behaves in such a way, then we are clearly having an issue. Oh, who am I kidding? Even if she's not behaving in an inappropriate way, I ain't having it and that will be known. Trust me. I am working on this one for sure, but I did tell y'all that I was going to be transparent so that's what I am doing.

Although this may be my reaction, jealousy shows itself in many different ways and in so many different scenarios. Jealousy does not only show up in romantic relationships; it can also show up in friendships, work environments, and even in families. We may have had that one coworker who just does everything right and you are completely over it. You may know your significant other has a "type" and it's nothing like you. And every time you see this "type," it sets you off. You may have a family member who can do no wrong and is favored by all, and then there's you, the black sheep, who can do nothing right.

Yes, all of these situations can cause jealousy to rear its ugly head and, in every scenario, it is still wrong. It started from the beginning with Cain and Abel. Cain killed his brother Abel out of jealousy. He was jealous that Abel was the one who was "favored" by God and because of this, he decided to kill him. If you are familiar with this story, then you know the truth. God was accepting of Abel and not of Cain, because Abel was obedient to God's orders and Cain was not.

At times we tend to overlook the truth when it comes to our feelings and how we perceive different situations that we may face. This is why I believe it is extremely important to go to God first when we start to feel something is amiss and ask Him to give us full wisdom on the real truth of the matter. He will, trust me. It is a promise in his Word after all. James 1:5: *"If any of you needs wisdom, ask our generous God, and He will give it to you. He will not rebuke you for asking."* Straight from the Word. He wants us to go to Him and ask Him what the truth really is. Once we know the truth, then we can act accordingly.

The enemy wants nothing more than to distort the truth. In doing so, our feelings will not be correct. We will then act on those feelings with an incorrect response, and it will not end well for anyone. Jealousy can cause a great deal of mess, believe you me, and it is not good at all for any type of relationship or even just for ourselves.

The Bible tells us about this ugly characteristic. (ESV) James 3:16 *"For where jealousy and selfish ambition exist, there will be disorder and every vile practice."* Yikes! How about this little lovely? Proverbs 14:30 *"A tranquil heart gives life to the flesh, but envy makes the bones rot."*

Of course, there are many more things God has to say about this word, but I think we get the point now. There is something to be said about the way God feels about this very common characteristic. Sad when you think about it, huh? Most things God hates are the things that we can so easily do. I now understand when the Apostle Paul meant when he stated in Romans 7:15 *"I do not understand what I do. For what I want to do I do not do, but what I hate I do."*

Wow, that's something. Here we have probably the greatest Apostle, telling us that he knew all he was to do and yet he did not do it. He still did what he knew was wrong. O.M.G. That is exactly how we are. It all comes down to our flesh. That nasty little sinful nature that we were all born with. Yeah, let's blame that. I mean, it wasn't our choice to be born with it. Ha! True, but it is our choice to decide to go against it. It's not easy, not by any means, but with God it sure is possible.

Next up, being boastful and proud. When most of us hear these words, we think about someone who is pretty much all about themselves. They are also all about letting everyone know it. The definitions are pretty much the same in meaning. Boastful: *"Showing excessive pride and self-satisfaction in one's achievements, possessions, or abilities."* Pride: *"A feeling of deep pleasure or satisfaction derived from one's own achievements."* Of course, taking pride in oneself and in what one achieves is fine, but it can quickly become behavior that is self-centered and prideful.

We must remain humble, and we must realize that, even though we may take pride in certain things we do or certain accomplishments, we can't forget that it is never of our own doing. It is God Himself who has blessed us with the abilities it took to accomplish such things, so the glory should always go to Him and never to ourselves.

God makes it clear in His Word that He does not take too kindly to pride. Proverbs 16: 5: *"The Lord detests the proud; they will surely be punished."* I don't know about you, but God is so loving, kind, and full of patience that, when He uses words like detest and surely, I know He isn't playing games.

The Word has many things to say about being boastful and prideful, and none of them are good. Actually, it is quite the opposite. God wants nothing to do with either of these traits, and He will deal harshly with anyone who carries these actions in their hearts.

Let's be honest, no one really likes to be around anyone who acts this way. How can we be called to be the light of the world and yet no one even desires to ever be near us? What good will we be then? To be honest, we are not much of a beacon of light at all with these types of characteristics being displayed. I mean who wants to be around someone who is constantly bragging about themselves and talking about themselves? I guarantee you, no one except the one who is bragging.

Being rude is in the same category. Rude: *"Offensively impolite or ill-mannered."* No one wants to be treated in this fashion, and those who tend to be rude rarely have many good and faithful friends because of it. Once again, how can we be called to be the light if there is no one around us to shine for? We may not constantly act out in these ways, but even just once and we are guilty.

We all have these negative traits in us because none of us were born perfect, but that is exactly why God sent His only Son to die for us so that we can live free of sin. None of us will ever perfect any of these traits here on earth, but that is not what God is asking of us. He knows we can't be perfect, and He doesn't expect perfection from us. All He wants from us is our hearts and the desire to do His will and to please Him. We must remember what the Word says about this. It is promised in the Word that we can do anything through Christ, who gives us strength.

Philippians 4:13. *I can do all things through Christ which strengtheneth me.* Being rude is extremely hurtful to others and that is pretty much the opposite of loving them if we want to be honest about it. There are so many people that are ill-mannered nowadays. It is sad. The amount of rampant selfishness and ugliness in today's society is overwhelming.

When someone is genuinely loving and kind, most people

tend to look at them as the weird ones. Some people view such kindness as totally foreign. Sad, isn't it? To not even recognize true kindness when it stares you in the face. How hurt God must be when He looks down at all of this nonsense going on today.

The devil is a liar, and yet we are giving him full permission to take over and run wild. It is the choices we make that say yes to him and his disgustingly foul nonsense. It is easy for us to look at someone who does something terrible and judge them. Sin is sin, and God sees it and it hurts Him. Especially when our actions hurt other people. No matter what we may feel about others, they are God's children, and He made them just like He made us. And He loves them just as much, so when we hurt other people, we are actually hurting God.

Chapter Three
DEMANDING? WHO, ME?

Have you ever been in a situation in which you knew — I mean you seriously knew beyond a shadow of a doubt — that the way you wanted to do something was the best way and clearly the fastest, yet the other person involved in the situation, who had no experience in this area whatsoever, swore you were wrong and they were right? You had the facts to prove it and you had done this task so many times before and yet this person still wanted to argue about it.

This type of situation can be quite irritating, especially if you have the receipts to prove it. There is no better feeling for us than to put a smackdown on a situation with full-blown receipts and end it with a dramatic mic drop, blow some air out your mouth, raise that left eyebrow, roll them eyes and neck at the same time, turn around with much attitude and walk away. Okay, maybe that's just me, but in any case, yep, you guessed it . . . Wrong again! Well, what do you think the Bible says about this one?

I am so glad you would like to know, so I will tell you. It says, *Love does not demand its own way.* Are you serious? I mean what if we are clearly right and everyone knows it except this one person who wants to challenge me? You mean to tell me, God expects me to just hush it and allow this person to "think" they are right, and I am supposed to do something their way and just act like nothing? How can that even be? Well, if we are followers of Christ and we are supposed to walk in His image, then we are not to be arguing with anyone.

Now, if anyone ever had the right to argue with people, especially knowing full well He is never wrong, it would be Jesus. And yet He never did. Arguing was not something He was about, and we are commanded to follow in His likeness. I am not saying you should simply be a doormat to everyone about anything they say. Being followers of Christ, if we are having any type of issue with anyone and we cannot decide what the right way to handle it may be, we must take it to the Lord, and He will give us the wisdom we need to handle it properly. It may not be in a way we would choose or even in our timing, but I can assure you, He will guide you in the truth on what to do and when.

Let me tell you a little secret. I am in no way a pastor, scholar, prophet, or anything other than a regular person, but in all of my experiences with God Himself, He sure has a way of using these situations to turn the tables and shine the light on you. This happens so many times when I go to Him with issues that now, instead of highlighting what the other person did, I go straight to Him and ask, *"Alright, Lord, what is it that I need to fix in me or what lesson are you trying to teach me in this situation?"*

On another note regarding this aspect of love, there is nothing wrong with voicing our opinions or standing up for what we believe is right. We simply must be careful that we are not doing it in our feelings, but we are doing it in *love* and not pushing it if it does not go our way. We should respect the opinions of others as well, regardless of whether we think we are right.

Jesus always did everything with *love,* and that is what changed people. I guarantee you this, no matter how nasty and mean someone can be, if you *love* on them and continue to no matter what, they will end up caving in and being nice to you in some sort of way, even if it is just to you and most of the time, you will end up being really loved and respected by them even if they don't say it out loud. Trust me, I have tested it many times. Look at it as a challenge when someone is not very kind. *Love* them. Continue to do it, and you will see changes happen.

This next one is a real doozy. I know I say that about most of them but that should just prove to you that I am in the same boat as everyone else. Wait, my boat may be a little more full than most, but either way, I am a work in progress and will be until my Father takes me home, and I am okay with that as long as I keep moving forward after I fall.

God looks at your heart and your progress; He is never looking for perfection. *"Love is not irritable."* Ha! The first thing that came to my mind when I saw this was, *OMG, I even irritate myself at times.* That can't be good. Let's look at this word together. Irritable: *"Having or showing a tendency to be easily annoyed or made angry."*

I could have seriously believed that my name was at the end of this definition. Funny how much you think you know about something until you really put the effort into studying it. As I began to really beat myself up about this one, God showed me how our society as a whole has a really bad time in this area. We have been so consumed by so many things that our stress level is way beyond where it should be. Therefore, most of us are constantly living on the edge. We worry about work, finances, our families, health issues, and our world. I mean, it's everywhere.

Turn on the news, and I guarantee you will be worried or bothered about some kind of an issue. God revealed to me in such a loving way that He did not design us to carry all of this stress and worry. This is exactly why He tells us in Philippians 4:6-7: *"Don't worry about anything; instead, pray about everything. Tell God what you need and thank Him for all He has done. Then you will experience God's peace, which exceeds anything we can understand. His peace will guard your hearts and minds as you live in Christ Jesus."*

This verse says quite a bit. God is telling us from His own Word that we have nothing to worry about because He is there to take it from us. What He told me was that the issue we are all having is that we are still stressed for one of two reasons. First off, there are those of us who are not giving our stresses and burdens to Him, and we are struggling to hold it all together by ourselves. This is just a ticking time bomb waiting to explode. And trust me, it will. It may not necessarily explode in anger, but it can manifest anywhere — your health, your mood, your work — literally anywhere. We were not built to carry that kind of weight and pressure.

Second, there are those of us who do call upon God. He takes it from us and we eventually go back and pick it right back up again. As I stated before, God loves us so much, He will at times let us have what we persist in having. He is always there to help us, but we need to be willing to call upon Him and ask Him for help. He longs for us to reach out to Him, because He wants nothing more than to help us and make our lives better. He will never force it upon us, however. He just sits and waits patiently.

The enemy wants nothing more than to use anything he can to keep us irritable. I mean, how can we show *love* to anyone if we are constantly snapping at people? On the other hand, how can we receive *love* if we do not want to be around people because they irritate us?

You see how the enemy uses all these tactics to keep us from doing what God has asked of us in His Word. It is crazy once you put it in that perspective, isn't it?

There are countless distractions and the tactics that the enemy uses on us from day to day, and yet we are so oblivious to them, and we are so accustomed to them that we even think they are the norm. However, the truth is far from that.

God tells us what we need to do about situations, as in 2 Corinthians 4:18: *"So we don't look at the troubles we can see now; rather, we fix our gaze on things that cannot be seen. For the things we see now will soon be gone, but the things we cannot see will last forever."*

Do you now understand why it is so important to have a personal relationship with God and to personally study His Word? He will reveal so much to you during this time. The things He will reveal to you, you cannot receive in a church sermon, a book, from a pastor, etc. His revelations will only be available to you in your personal relationship with God Himself. This is exactly why just going to church on Sundays, or going to every meeting under the sun, or even listening to every podcast known to man will never replace your personal relationship and alone time with the Father.

I know it may seem weird and even boring at first, but I promise you this: once you start, it will be so incredible you will desire it constantly and it will be the one thing in your life you will refuse to give up. You will need to protect it daily and feed into it, because the enemy, Satan himself, knows how important and powerful that relationship is to you, and he will do whatever it takes to distract you and keep you from it.

If Satan can remove your relationship with God, then he can remove your power and authority against him and his demons. He is very strategic about how he plans his attacks on us, because he knows exactly what will catch our attention and what our weaknesses are, and you'd better believe he will use anything and everything to keep you from your power. This is exactly why we need to be walking in wisdom and discernment, rather than in these oblivious states that most of us are in — so preoccupied with the things of this world we have no time for the things we were actually put on this earth for, God's purpose for us.

There are many things today that we do on the norm that will automatically put us into an irritable state. At the end of our day, after work and everything else we put on our plates, how many of us are still even functioning properly let alone doing it with a good attitude. Do you tend to ignore your spouse or your kids because you are just too tired to do otherwise? Do you have time for the dog, or does his constant whining irritate you even more than you already are when you think about it. All he or she wants to do is be with you because they *love* you so much.

Being irritable and overwhelmed does more than steal our joy, it depletes us of the *love* that we are designed for. The *love* and closeness of others are the exact things that should be bringing us joy. Think about how it was in the beginning of most things. What I mean by that is a relationship, for example. Most everyone is so head over heels and in *"love"* that we want nothing more than to be with that person 24/7. All of the cute conversations and the closeness and time spent. Now after you have been together or married for a bit, what actually happens and why have things changed so that they are no longer as they were? How is *love* lost?

Well, most of us never had that real *love* to begin with so that is the first real issue. Second, we got so used to having it that it just doesn't mean as much to us anymore. How sad is that? Having the exact same thing that some of us prayed for and just couldn't do without, and now we don't even see it as important and tend to even see it as burdensome now.

This is exactly what emotions can do and that is why God tells us not to go by them, because they are not reliable and can change at the drop of a hat. True *Love*, however, will never change. Imagine you losing that spouse, that child, or even that dog. Think about how you would feel then. I am sure that, if you really do care for them, then it would be devastating to even think about, but if it doesn't bother you much then you know you made the wrong choice to begin with.

Crazy when you really stop and think about these things in depth, right? This is exactly why the enemy strives to keep our minds distracted by so many other things. Our phones, jobs, social media, even church, friends, family, and even good things can be used to distract us from what God has actually called us to do. Our joy will never be full, and we will never feel truly satisfied in life until we are actually in the purpose that God has called us to be in.

We each have our own purpose in His plan while we are here. That is why it is so important to be with the spouse that He has hand-picked for us. They are already set up to be a part of our purpose as well. If we are not obedient and choose whoever we feel is right, then we only make it so much harder for ourselves.

Remember, He knows what's best for us, and anything else is just not good enough. I don't know about you, but I am tired of mediocrity. I want the best. His best.

Chapter Four

KEEPING RECORD? WHO, ME?

Nothing bothers me more when I am trying to communicate my feelings to someone, in order to let them know that what they did or said to hurt me, than when the first thing they say is, "Well, you did this and last time you said . . ."

Seriously? We are not even talking about that at this time, and I thought we had already resolved the issue when it had happened years ago, yet you continue to bring it up every single time we have any kind of an issue. Don't get me wrong. We all do this, even if we don't say the words aloud. It is not okay.

We may think to ourselves, *no, he/she didn't just bring that up again. You know how many times I kept quiet about all of these things I've been holding in. One day, I promise you, I am not going to be so nice.*

This, my friend, is no different than the other. Both are equally wrong in God's eyes.

I am sure you may have guessed it by now, but the next thing the Bible says about *love* is that *Love keeps no record of being wronged.*

The actual definition of Keeping Record is this: *"The act or process of creating and maintaining records, archiving."*

When I asked God about this one, He told me it isn't much

deeper than what it seems. You see, it's not just the simple act of remembering certain situations; it is the act of purposefully keeping record and remembering certain situations, and then actually filing them in a certain place in your mind with the intent of using them in the future. Now you may say to yourself, *"I would never say anything about that again."*

However true this may be, the fact that you took the time to specifically take these situations, separate them out, and place them in a part of your mind where you can remember them and use them as needed is *so* not okay. Just because you do not say them out loud, does not mean you will not use them in the future. You see, the enemy knows that you have hidden those specific thoughts away and, believe you me, he can and will get you to use them. You may not say anything out loud, but because they are there and locked and loaded — just in case — you'd better believe the devil will strike with the *"just in case."*

Keeping these situations in your mind will help you to remember them at different times, thus altering your attitude toward that person at some time or another. This will become more and more present as time goes on. The enemy is so slick, you will not even realize it is happening until you can't stand this person and you have no idea why.

This is exactly why staying in a close relationship with the Father is so important. It is in this close relationship that the Holy Spirit will prompt you in some way, or even many different ways depending on how quickly we catch on, to make you aware of what's really going on. He will do this so that we can be aware and fix things before they begin to take root in our hearts. Uprooting issues from our hearts is difficult, but we can remove and heal. God will have the Holy Spirit prompt us so that we catch these types of things, deal with them from the beginning, and be done with it once and for all.

If we are not in that personal relationship with Him, and if we are not speaking to Him on a daily basis, then we will not be able to hear His voice, which is exactly where the enemy wants us to be. He works his best when we are separated from the Father. You see, something that I heard once really resonated with me. It was this: The Lord always whispers, and the enemy shouts. This is exactly why we can hear the enemy so much more clearly than the Lord, unless we have an intimate relationship with Him. If we have that type of relationship with the Father then no matter how loud the shouting gets, our spirit will always hear the Holy Spirit's whispers.

Next up is all about truth. *"Love does not rejoice about injustice but rejoices whenever the truth wins out."* Injustice is defined as the lack of fairness and fairness is defined as *"impartial and just treatment or behavior without favoritism or discrimination."*

It is safe to say that a lack of fairness would occur when someone is not treated justly because of favoritism or discrimination. This one is huge in our world today. This is a subject that I am not, nor have I ever been, comfortable discussing. I feel this way because so many people believe differently, and this subject matter can be very touchy. Oh, and you'd better believe a touchy situation, especially among believers and non-believers, is the devil's playground. He loves to manipulate these types of situations and in so many ways.

Politics can be the breeding ground for chaos and misunderstandings, and we all know what can come about in these types of situations, i.e., anger, hate, resentment, separation, destruction, and sadly, it can go even further than that at times. It can go to the extreme in some cases and even have lifelong repercussions. Think about that one for a moment.

A situation that starts off with "injustice" immediately divides people. Who loves to cause division? John 10:10: *"The thief's purpose is to steal, kill and destroy.* As soon as this occurs, you see the two sides that begin to form. One side argues about the injustice and the other side defends it. Anger spikes. The situation escalates quickly. Once anger becomes part of the equation, it is pretty much inevitable that the outcome will have lifelong repercussions for at least one, if not many people.

I am sure you don't have an issue believing me on this one. If you do, all you have to do is turn on the news, watch it for a short period of time, and you will see exactly what I am talking about. It is everywhere these days — in schools, jobs, sports, the government, of course, in our leadership and yes, even in our churches. This saddens me.

Do you see what "living in our feelings" can do to us and cause for others? This is exactly why the enemy loves for us to live in our feelings, and He will cause situations to occur just to sit back and enjoy the chaos.

Now, do not get me wrong. The enemy does not cause every bad thing that happens in life; there can be a number of things that cause them. Bad choices, unexpected circumstances, other people's choices and get this one, even God. Yes, God can allow us to go through the fire in order to shape us into the mighty men and women of God He intends for us to be. This is yet another reason why we need to stay in a close relationship with Him. He will let us know what to do in every situation, and how, but we will never know unless we are in constant communication with Him.

Are you starting to see the value and importance of being in that close relationship with God? If not, then anything can happen. We are fair game. I used to tell my babies when they were young that being under God's protection was like standing under this big umbrella. As long as we were under there, we would be protected. The devil was like a roaring lion seeking whom he might devour, as per the Word. I told them that it was like a big lion pacing back and forth all around the umbrella, just waiting for one hair of ours to go over the perimeter. That was all it would take for him to grab hold and drag us right out from under the protective covering.

I also told them that the closer we got to sin and doing things not of God, the closer we would get to the perimeter of the umbrella. It's best not to play with things like that and to stay all the way in God's will by remaining in the middle and completely covered.

It is never a good thing to play with boundaries, thinking that we know better and would never go all the way. Ha! Yet another one of the enemy's lovely lies.

You will always get into trouble when you play with fire. We must never underestimate the power of the enemy. Yes, Our Lord has all of the power and wins every time. However, that same power and authority cannot be used if we are in sin and not where we are supposed to be.

I know you are probably thinking, *Okay, this is all just overwhelming and how am I supposed to figure all of this out?*

I say this because it is what I thought a great deal of the time. I am at the point in my journey where I can stop myself once I begin to feel this way and recognize that this is not how the Lord wants me to feel. Remember, God is not a God of confusion. 1 Corinthians 14:33: *"For God is not a God of confusion but of peace..."* This verse immediately reminds me that once I start to entertain confusion, I am no longer in the will of God. And when we are not in the will of God, all sorts of things can happen and most of them are not good.

All of this can be a lot to take in, but remember there is only one thing you need to hang onto and that is the fact that you do not have to do any of this on your own. This is exactly why your personal relationship with God is so important. You will not have to worry about anything, because He has given us His Holy Spirit to help and guide us in everything we encounter.

Yes, *anything* we may face or have issues with, *anything* at all. He will guide us through and provide everything we need. This is why the Bible says, we do not have to worry. Matthew 6:26: *"Look at the birds. They don't plant or harvest corn store food in barns, for your heavenly Father feeds them. And aren't you far more valuable to Him than they are?"*

And let us not forget verse 30. The Bible is full of promises and truths, which is why we must read it, study it, and do what it says — daily. As I am reading this passage, I become so filled with joy and excitement, I want to write it all down, even though I cannot rewrite the entire Bible. You are blessed to have access to the Bible. So, pick it up and read it anytime you choose, and I guarantee that your life will change dramatically.

Matthew 6:28-31 *"And why worry about your clothing? Look at the lilies of the field and how they grow. They don't work or make their clothing, yet Solomon and all of his glory was not dressed as beautifully as they are. And if God cares so wonderfully for wildflowers that are here today and thrown into the fire tomorrow, He will certainly care for you. Why do you have so little faith?"*

I know you may hear this a lot but I promise you, when we hear things over and over, it is usually something we need to pay close attention to. God loves each of us so very much, He sent His only son to die for us so that we can be with Him for all eternity. He sent His own son to take the beatings, the lashings, the ridicule, and all of the other pain and suffering so you would not need to endure these injustices.

I know we hear this a lot, and we tend to just run right past it, but I want you to really stop and meditate on this for a minute. This is exactly what I did, and it was as if the lightbulb finally turned on after countless years.

I am a very visual person, so I tend to visualize things in order to get a better perspective. Now I have two boys of my own and everyone, and I mean everyone, knows how much I *love* my babies. I have a baby girl, too, and she is my heart. Yes, they are all grown now, but they are still mama's babies.

Knowing how much these babies mean to me and knowing full well that I will certainly forget everything I am writing to you if someone would even think of harming them, I would NEVER, EVER even think to sacrifice any of them for ANYONE, let alone selfish, sinful and ungrateful people like us. Sounds harsh, but it is the truth. We are born this way. And we will be this way until we accept Christ and believe that He died for us so that we would no longer be selfish, sinful, and ungrateful people.

Let that marinate for a bit. Close your eyes for a moment. Think about your child, your parents, your significant other, even yourself. Whoever you love more than anything. Now that you have their images in your mind, I want you to think about them being whipped, beaten to near death right in front of you, and all you can do is watch. You can't yell, fight, or even cry out . . . you simply watch in horror.

Now I want you to picture them being dragged, kicked, spit on, and made to carry the heaviest load all while they (or you) are bleeding and broken and grasping the final threads of what little life they have left in them. Then, as they are walking, you see an opportunity to run to them and face them one last time. As you look them in the eye, you cannot even speak while they look at you with what little breath they can muster and they say, "It's okay, Mama, I'm making it all better."

I don't know about you but just writing this and thinking about it is difficult for me. I am in tears as I write. When I asked God to help me to understand How much He loves me, this is the exact vision He gave me and it changed my life forever. He loves us all this much. I don't know about you, but that does something to my heart and my spirit. We will dig deeper into this later, but look at the injustice in that entire situation. Watch any movie about the Resurrection, and you will see the injustice. The Passion of the Christ will do it, I promise you.

When I saw the following quote, it touched my heart. *"Until I truly understand what Jesus did on the cross, I cannot truly understand why my commitment to what is right must take priority over what I prefer."* Not sure who came up with this, but it is so true.

Injustice is not of God, and those of us who support injustice for any reason are not living as God has called us to. Once again, we go back to the relationship with God. If you are not sure about something, then go straight to Him and ask Him about it. He will surely tell you, and then you will be certain you will be walking in truth after that. No matter what anyone else says, what God tells you is what stands. Period. *"Love rejoices whenever the truth wins out."*

Really, what is truth? There are so many verses in the Word that talk about truth.

John 14:6: *Jesus told him, "I am the way, the truth, and the life. No one can come to the Father except through me."*

John 17:17: (ESV) *Sanctify them in the truth; your Word is truth.*

John 8:31-32: *Jesus said to the people who believed in Him, "You are truly my disciples if you remain faithful to my teachings. And you will know the truth and the truth will set you free."*

There are many more beautiful verses on truth, yet these few say it all. As we look over the verses, and also look back on what God says about *Love* and truth, we see that *"Love rejoices whenever the truth wins out."*

Truth, as we now see, is the Living Word of God. Not only is it the Word of God, truth is God. He said it in John 14:6. *He is the way, the truth, and the life.* So, what this is saying to us is that *Love* rejoices when God's way wins out. If two people are in an altercation, we automatically know that such behavior is not God's will. Therefore, we should not be standing by, watching, recording on our phones, and commentating as we post the video on social media. Not participating in the situation does not mean we aren't involved.

How about laughing at someone else's pain? What may seem funny to us may be completely embarrassing to someone else, and the consequences of everyone laughing and constantly bringing it up may cause someone severe anxiety or some other type of negative reaction. We may think we know someone very well and for many years, but no matter what we may think, no one knows what anyone is really feeling inside.

Only God knows the heart. And He knows our hearts even better than we know our own. So just because we may think it's nothing to someone, we really have no idea what they feel inside and for this reason, we must be vigilant on how our actions may affect someone else. If we try to live our best lives, as God has called us to, then we would all be living in a world nothing like we see now.

You may be saying to yourself, "Well, I am only one person and even if I try my best, what can only one person do? Please let me tell you. I know the exact answer to this question because I, too, asked God the exact same one and He said to me, *"One person can save an entire nation. Just look at Abraham."*

Well, that just shut me up real quick, didn't it? God plays no games whatsoever when you talk to Him. He wants nothing more than to communicate with you. That is actually something He really desires.

Chapter Five
NOT MY WILL BUT HIS

Who would have thought one little passage on *love* could be so detailed and so packed with knowledge? I mean, when I first started to write this book, I had a whole different plan in mind. I wanted to just talk about this verse a bit in Chapter One and then move on from there, yet God had a whole different plan in mind. I *love it* when I think I have it all together, and then God just nonchalantly comes along and changes the entire scene.

I remember in the beginning of my relationship with Him, this sort of thing used to set me off. I mean, I was an extreme perfectionist and total control freak about my life. Everything needed to go by the book. Now, I just laugh and say, *"Okay, God, let's do this."* I praise God every day that I can do this now, because I have gone through so much with Him. Now I know for a fact that when He changes things, it is ALWAYS for my good and the good of others as well. Who doesn't want that?

The stress is no longer present, and I know everything will turn out exactly the way God wants it to. That is enough for me. Is it always just that simple? It can be, yes, but ultimately, it is my decision. It is completely up to me to surrender it all to God and allow Him to handle it in the best way, or I can decide to keep picking it up, stressing myself out, holding onto control and simply prolonging the process. Remember, He never forces us to do anything. God is a complete gentleman.

Next up is one of my FAVORITES!!! I say this because it is finally something I am good at. Not perfect, by any means, but with God I can tackle this one most days with a smile on my face. Don't get me wrong. It is very difficult and at times almost impossible but once again, "With God."

One of my gifts from God is my strength. I am pretty strong both physically and mentally, but the mental strength I have is not the norm. I promise it is actually a weakness of mine, God works best in our weaknesses. It took me up until pretty recently to figure this one out. The enemy does not want us to see our strengths. And trust me when I say, he will do anything to camouflage them. I have gone through some things in my life that would take out pretty much anyone and almost myself, as well, yet God came through. That is a whole other book. Or as my kids would say, *"A series of novels."* Ha. Ha. Ha.

LOVE NEVER GIVES UP! This means more to me than most. It has so many different significant situations attached to it for me that just writing the words has me in tears. First off, let's see what the meaning of *"giving up"* is.

There are two definitions that grip my heart so let's look at them together. 1. Giving up: *cease making an effort; resign oneself to failure.* (Admit defeat) 2. Giving up: *allow oneself to be taken over by an emotion or addiction. "He gave himself up to pleasure."*

Once again, I could write an entire book on these two definitions alone. These hit me so hard and in so many ways. Anyone who knows me realizes I can be pretty — ummm — let's say persistent when I want something, and I will do pretty much whatever it takes to get it. I can also be extremely competitive. Just ask my son. He will never let me forget the time I *"pushed him into the wall with my go-cart . . ."* I really don't think it happened this way, but I did smoke everyone that I was with. Just saying. (This happened not very long ago.) So, it is safe to say that I hate failing and yet I find it so funny how something that I hate so much can happen so often.

The pure thought of failing just upsets me, and when I look at this definition and see that it says to stop even trying and pretty much give in to failure, that is just mind-blowing to me. You are basically choosing to quit and give up. As upsetting as it sounds to me, I have been there and I completely understand. It is a feeling of no control, no other choice but to give in and quit. This, my friends, is a lie from the enemy, and it is exactly what he wants you to think and to do. He wants and needs you to give up. He needs this because when we give up, we are no longer in the mindset of doing God's will and fulfilling His purpose for us in our lives.

When this happens, we are in selfish mode. Yep, I said it. "Selfish mode." We don't think about all of the other people who will be affected in a positive way and who are waiting for us to do God's will. Take Moses, for example. He did not want to do what God called him to do, so he delayed. The Israelites had to wait on him. He gave excuses to God as to why he should not be the one called to take on this mighty task, and he told God all about his failures and faults. Ha! Isn't that so like us when we do not think we can do something? We point out our own flaws, and we fail ourselves before we even begin to try.

God already knows everything about us, He made us. Remember? He knows exactly what we can do and can't do. He has already equipped us to do what He has called us to do even if we do not think so. Think about the time wasted while Moses tried to get out of God's will and at the same time many were suffering and praying for a deliverer.

This also happened with Jonah. He refused to go to Nineveh. He ran from God, and he ended up in the belly of the fish. But after all this nonsense and extreme stress, which he brought on himself, he did exactly what God willed anyway. Isn't this behavior just like us? We do what we want and when it doesn't work, we get upset. We might even blame God, and we keep doing the same things until we finally get tired. Obedience is so important. We were not made to quit or to give up on anything that God has called us to do, no matter how difficult it may seem. God will always equip us to do what He has called us to do. Oh, and one more thing, God's will doesn't change. It will happen so we might as well just get into it the first time around.

Now, let's talk a bit about the part of the definition which talks about being taken over by emotion or addiction. We all know how tough it is to fight against any strong emotions we may feel. Especially feelings of anger, pain, defeat, guilt, shame, etc. When we allow our emotions to rule us, there is no telling how deep we can spiral down and how quickly it can happen. It is usually at this point that all we can do is focus on our feelings and nothing else. This is when quitting can become the only option we may see. The enemy loves to get us to this point because once we are here, he does not have to do much but watch us do it all ourselves.

Let me tell you a little something about myself. I am the queen of living in my feelings. Oh, yes. This has been an issue with me since birth. I can take one little word that someone says and turn it into a whole Broadway play in my mind in a matter of seconds and my emotions are going nuts about it. Let's just say that there was a time that popping off was a way of life for me.

If I felt some type of way, someone was going to hear about it. If I didn't like something, everyone would know. And if I felt upset enough to want to knock someone out . . . unfortunately, I would. I would just do whatever I felt, then deal with the consequences after the fact.

Yes, I just threw a load of my dirty laundry out for y'all to see, because I want you to understand how God can use what we have used in a negative way and turn it around for His Glory. This is embarrassing for me to write about now, especially because of how I feel about God at this point in my life. I used to be so stupid and proud of myself back then because I could hold my own and fight anyone who stepped up. I could take on anything, yet I was a complete mess inside. Broken to my core and no one ever knew it. Except, of course, God.

God knew because He is the one who made me and He did so with all of my flaws included. He knew I would need them, and He would use them for my good. Despite all the mistakes I would make, God knew what would happen and He NEVER GAVE UP on me. He rescued me, and He will do the same for you.

Am I perfect? Heck, no! Not even close. I still struggle with all of this daily, but it is nothing like it was before. I feel so free from all of the garbage that I held inside for years. The pain, the secrets, the brokenness, the unspoken shame and the guilt. It was torture and there were things I held in my heart that I did not even know about until God revealed them to me. This can all be achieved just by walking with God and allowing Him to take over.

I remember when I was told to allow God to take over and He would fix everything. My response? *Uh, no thank you. I mean, I love God for sure, but I am not trying to be this holy person who goes around preaching and irritating people. I don't want to be in church for hours at a time and praying for hours. I don't want to stop listening to my music and doing the things I love, either.*

Ha! Yep, I said those words. Now, I have to laugh. Looking back, it was a lie from the devil because it isn't that way at all. Yes, there are changes that happen but it's because I wanted them to happen, and I chose to do them. Nothing was ever forced on me, and God will never force anything on you either. He is not this angry judgmental God who sits on his throne with a hammer, waiting to smack us when we sin. Yes, that is how I pictured Him to be when I was growing up. The whole *God's gonna punish you* kind of thing. Nope, not the God I serve, I promise you!

My God is a loving and forgiving Father, and He loves me more than anyone. I am His child. He made me exactly as I am, and He loves me that way. He just wants to refine me a bit so that I can shine so much more and help others to shine, too! He loves you in just the same way, and He wants to do the exact same thing for you.

I want to look at two words that really do have a huge impact when we do choose to give up or quit. The words are *failure* and *defeat*. Let's talk about these words for a second. These are two words that I hate, especially if I can help it. It's one thing to try and then fail, but it's another thing to fail because of giving up or *"ceasing to make an effort."* Failing is tough either way, but to fail because you gave up or didn't even try is horrible in my mind.

The first thing I think of is *what if?* What if I would have kept trying? What if I did succeed? What if I would have . . .? Oh the torture of the *"what-ifs"*. At least if you try your best with anything and it doesn't work out, then it's okay because you gave it your all. Although I have learned that failure isn't that common for me as much now. If you take everything to God, He tells you what to do, and you are obedient, then even if it doesn't work out the way you wanted it to, it still is not a failure because God's way never fails. We win. Now I can say with confidence that I am no longer a failure, nor will I ever be a failure as long as I stay in God's will and am obedient to what He tells me.

Let's return to the emotions and addictions part once again. It is striking, because it talks about being taken over by our emotions or addictions. I know most of us see the word addictions and our minds automatically run to alcohol and drug use. Yes, these can be additions for some, yet these are not the only additions we can possess.

Re-examine the word *addiction* for a moment. Addiction: *"The fact or condition of being addicted to a particular substance, thing, or activity."*

There you have it: *a thing or an activity*. This changes the whole game on this word. Yes, there are some of us who are addicted to substances, yet there are many more of us who are addicted to things and activities.

You don't think so? Let's see. What about your job? Your

significant other? Your money? Your business? Your material things? What about your family? Your church?

Yep, they don't necessarily have to be bad things we are addicted to, but we can allow them to take over everything else in our lives. For example, I was addicted to living in my feelings. It determined the way I lived, reacted to things, my mood, and so much more. We do not understand that anything we are addicted to really does have a negative effect on us and the people around us. It has even more of an impact on those we *love* most.

What we are addicted to is usually what we put at the core or the center of our lives. Nothing should be at the core of our lives but God. God actually designed us to work best when He is at the center of our lives. You don't think so, then take a look at what the Word says.

John 15:7 *"If you remain in me and my words remain in you, ask whatever you wish, and it will be done for you."* O.M.G. Do you know what this means? This is huge. This is saying that if you just put God first and be obedient to all He says in the word, which is pretty much to *love* people, then you can believe He will take care of you and give you your heart's desires. When you do this, your true desires will no longer be the same desires you had when you were led by the world and the Father of Lies.

When you put God at the center, your heart changes. Your desires change, as well. They change for the better. And God will bless you above and beyond what you could ever think to ask of Him. You don't think so? Try Him. He will never fail you , as long as you are asking Him for the right reasons. He's the only one who truly knows your heart. He knows our hearts even better than we do.

Once we let go of our addictions and release all control to God, He will start to do great and mighty things for us. You will get to the point where you are not even sure what to do with yourself, because you will have so much peace through the storms, you will think something's wrong. I remember thinking,

Am I supposed to be worried right now? Because even though I am going through a storm, I feel at peace.

The feeling was crazy but then again, the Word does say in Phil. 4:6-7 *"Do not be anxious about anything, but in every situation, by prayer and petition, with thanksgiving, present your requests to God. And the peace of God, which transcends all understanding, will guard your hearts and minds in Christ Jesus."*

There you have it, straight from the Word. Why do we all have so much trouble doing this? The trouble comes from our stubborn and controlling flesh. We want control and we want what we want when we want it. We must discipline ourselves to change in order to really surrender everything to God. We may surrender everything to Him one minute and yet try to pick it up again in the next minute, so we must constantly renew our minds to the Word and not to what we feel or see. It is very difficult at first, but it will get better as we keep at it.

We will always need to work at it until the day He comes for us. It is so worth it because the blessings that come from this are tremendous. God never calls upon us to be perfect, He simply calls us to come just as we are and let Him take it from there. Once The Father is at the center, He will never allow you to give up, no matter how much you may feel you want to. He will always come in like a flood with His strength. He will renew you and you will suddenly have what it takes to keep moving forward.

Why? you may ask. Because you are relying on Him, and He will never ever fail you.

Chapter Six
CONFUSION NEVER IS FROM HIM

*L*ove never loses faith and is always hopeful. What does this even mean? Losing *faith* for what? And *hopeful* for what? This part was a bit confusing to me. I know I am to have faith in God, but faith in others? You already know people are not reliable, and it is hard enough for me to trust and have faith in God, who is a Man of His Word, and now you are asking me to have faith in something or someone other than Him? Ummmm. How about No! This was my first thought. I know, I know, but I am being honest as I told you all I would be.

And as far as hope is concerned . . . I mean, really? After all the times I have been burned, you still want me to hope and continue to hope, no matter what? *How many times are you expecting me to get hurt, Lord?* Geez, come on. It was at that moment when I remembered the story about Peter in the Bible when He asked Jesus, how many times was he expected to forgive?

Ha! Ha! Ha! Peter and I have many similarities. I mean, he was ready to fight, had anger issues and wanted to control everything. He was king of the pop-off . Well, I know exactly how that went. I bet he was floored when Jesus told him to forgive as many times as it takes. I can see Peter's face now. I am sure it was something like mine would have been. Lifted eyebrow and side eye as I said, "Seriously? Come on, Jesus. For real? How many times?" This is exactly what The Holy Spirit revealed to me when I asked about hope and how many times I would be hurt before I could let this one go.

What we do not understand — I know this because I did not understand it, either — is that there is no way any of us can do the things God asks of us without Him. In our human self, we can do nothing. We will fail every time because no one is perfect. No one. No matter how strong and how together you may think you are, no one is perfect. The only way we will be able to succeed at any of this is to have God at the core of our lives. When we do that, we invite Him in to have His way with us. The outcome is simply astounding.

There will be times that you feel like a superhero because it is God's strength you are feeling, not your own. There will also be the times of trial, yet we are to count it all joy like it tells us in James 1:2, because He is using the trials to grow us and make us even stronger but believe this, even through all of that, He is still right there with us just like Shadrach, Meshach, and Abednego in the middle of the fire. We must never forget, no matter how hot the fire was turned up on these boys, they all came out untouched and without a trace of even being near a furnace, let alone being in it. Oh, praise God for this!!!

This makes me want to scream out loud! I mean, think about that for a second. You may be going through what seems like pure Hell in your life, yet if you put your trust in God, you will make it out without even a blemish or trace of ever having been in the fire at all. The only thing you will see coming out is your faith being strengthened. Yes, Lord, give me that! This, my friends, is what is meant by the refining process. We all must endure it to get to where God has called us to be, yet we are never expected to go through it alone. He will always be with us. If we do not feel Him near, then we can be sure that it is not His doing but our own. He will never abandon or forsake us.

Now, let me make this part very clear because I wish I'd known this before my trials. Going through the fire and trusting God may not look like what you think, believe me. I remember thinking to myself, *are you kidding me? Do you even know what I am going through, and yet you want me to just let it all go, forget about it and skip through life and trust you, God, with no care about it at all?*

Ha! That is not at all what it looks like, especially not at first. I remember what it looked like for me, and mind you, everyone's journey with the Father is different, but mine was very . . . how should I say this? Dramatic! Remember, I am very vocal and a bit animated at times. Just a little.

My journey consisted of a great deal of sadness, anger, disappointment, screaming, yelling, and even cursing. My emotions ran all over the place, yet I never stopped praying and talking to God. I just took all of those feelings to Him, and I was completely honest. As I stated earlier, He already knows how I am feeling. And whether I say it out loud or not, He knows what's in my heart.

I know there are a lot of people who think it is just too much to go to God that way. I have had people gasp at me when I told them this, and I have had others tell me it was very disrespectful to talk to God in such a way. I do not feel this way. I am in no way cursing at God or talking disrespectfully to Him; I am simply expressing my feelings to Him. I may be mad, I may scream, I may curse (not anymore), but I was real. And I know that is how God wants us to go to Him.

After all, He made us and knows exactly how we are, so trust me when I say it will be no surprise to Him. Think about this for a second. I have mentioned this previously. If God wants to be our everything and He wants us to have the most intimate relationship with Him, and Him first, then why wouldn't He want us as pure and naked as possible? He wants us to come to Him just as we are. Once we do this, He will *love* us so completely, we will start to change our way of doing things. This only happens with Him and in His timing, not ours.

God will never come at us in an unloving and impatient way; that is not His character. Even when God does discipline us, He always does it in a loving way. Everything He does for us and to us is all for our good. We cannot compare Him to any relationship or person or circumstance that we know or have experienced, because He is unique. You may not understand it now, but as you grow closer to Him and spend more and more time with Him, you will surely see what I am talking about. All of this is a journey yet He is with you the entire way. It is not difficult. When you look back, trust me, you would do it all over again just to be that close to Him.

You will never want to go back to the way it was. When you start talking to Him on the daily, having those straight conversations during which you can literally ask Him something and He will answer you right back, it is simply amazing. I know because I have been through it all. I would go through the fire all over again just to gain this intimate relationship with Him. It is like nothing you can even imagine. You would give up everything just to keep it. Now I know exactly how the disciples must have felt. Being that close to Him is like nothing you have ever known.

All of this being said, when you have this type of relationship with the Father, it is so much easier with Him to have faith and hope in anything, because you know He is the one who holds you up and you will always be okay as long as you have Him as your core. What I mean by this is that, if you do put your hope and faith into other people since we are called to *love* everyone, when, and I do say *when* because they will, when they fail us, we will know that it will be okay. God has us and He will make it alright as long as we are in His will. We must make sure we are always obedient to Him and do what He asks of us.

Other people will always disappoint us, let us down, hurt us, and we will do the same to others as well. We may not even be aware of doing it and they may not be aware, either, but because not one of us is perfect, we will always make mistakes whether we mean to or not. This is why we do not put others at our core, we put God there because He will be the one to make it all work out for our good.

Trust me, I have gone through small fires on my own without Him that I thought were extremely devastating. On the other hand, I have gone through major traumas with God that felt nothing like the little fires I went through on my own. God gives us the strength we need to survive whatever comes our way — as long as we are doing our best to depend on Him and Him alone. He should be the first one we run to in every situation, good or bad. Every decision we make should be discussed with Him first.

Of course, it is good to get godly advice from other brothers and sisters in Christ. The word *"Christian"* does not mean anything. I hate to even say this, but what I have seen more often than not is that many people who claim the title of *"Christian"* have the worst fruit than those who don't. It's sad because they should know better. I know because that person used to be me. Once you receive advice from your brother or sister with good fruit, ALWAYS take it to God first. It doesn't matter who it is — a pastor, a great leader, a well-known person or just an amazing brother or sister in Christ. Everything always needs to be run by God first.

All of these people are just that, people. And every one of them was born in sin, so no matter how much we look up to them, they are not free of sin and mistakes. The devil can use anyone, and I mean *anyone*, to get you off God's will. The devil will do it.

Many of us have had pastors lead them astray, giving advice that was in complete opposition to what God was saying to them. I have experienced this firsthand. This is exactly why we need to have an intimate relationship with God, because when we take all of that to Him, He will surely show you the truth and fast. With me it was immediate. I was so amazed. When I began to thank Him, He told me that it was because of my obedience in coming to Him first and wanting Him to have the final say.

Jeremiah 29:13 is what I stand on to this day. *"You will seek me and find me when you seek me with all of your heart."*

We will all make mistakes on this journey, yet God does not expect perfection from us. He just wants us to choose Him. He knows our heart and its true intentions. If our heart is meaning to do right and we try our best, then that is enough for Him. We need to check our motives.

We can try to do everything right and be completely obedient to what He asks of us, yet if our motives are wrong then none of it matters. I don't know about you, but I am not the one who wants to hear, *"Depart from me for I never knew you."* Oh no, those words are not it, especially coming from God Himself. Can you imagine?

I am not sure about you, but I think it is so much easier to have faith and hope in other people when you consider how much faith and hope God has in us even when we make mistakes and fail constantly. We are to extend grace to others, and it really is so much easier to do so when we think about the grace God extends to us daily.

Right about now, some of you may be thinking, *what about these people that just keep hurting us and keep doing this and that? How are we supposed to keep loving them and extending grace over and over?*

Loving others and extending grace is what we are constantly called to do to everyone, but I must say, if you are living in constant communication with the Father then He will guide you in what decisions to make when it comes to each individual. Loving someone and extending grace does not necessarily mean continuing to hang out with them or continuing to be a punching bag for them.

If you go to God in every situation, He will show you what to do and how to do it. Trust me on this. Loving someone may not necessarily look the way you think. It may look like you are keeping quiet when you want to pop off, or it may look like you are praying for them from a distance or even having tough conversations with them but always in *love*. It can mean anything, but the only one who can tell you is God. His way is always the best way, even if you do not see it that way at first. You will see it that way in the end though.

Have you ever asked, even begged God for something you really wanted, and He didn't come through? You might have even been angry at Him because of it, then down the line you thought, OMG — *thank you, Lord, for not giving me that nonsense, I would have died. Please, Lord, do not listen to me ever.* Then you ask Him for something again later.

I have reached the point that I simply say to God, *"Look, I may think I want this, but in Jesus's Mighty Name, get it the heck away from me if it is not of you because I don't even want to look at it or think about it one second if you didn't mean it for me!"* I obviously learned most of my lessons the hard way.

Another great thing about never losing faith and always being hopeful when we *love* others is that we are always in a positive mindset. When we are in this mindset, it is very difficult for anything to shake us, especially since we know we are in God's will. When you know this, you can be confident that whatever comes your way, God has already had his hand on it and has prepared you for it in advance. Nothing shocks Him.

Clearly if you are talking to Him on the daily, and He is the one ordering your steps, then any situation that comes up has already got an answer. We just have to take it to Him to figure it out and simply obey what He tells us to do. It will come with challenges because we usually go straight to freak-out mode. Everything we know to do flies right out of the window, and most of us go right back to what we do best, i.e., worry, panic, trying to control the situation on our own, yet in time, we eventually learn to leave more and more of that behind and simply trust Him.

This is a process, and it takes time. Never beat yourself up because you didn't get it right away. We must remember, condemnation is never from God. God will convict us, but only to show us that we must try harder next time, or to warn us not to do something before we do it. The enemy will use anything He can to get us off of God's will, which is why we need to be grounded in God and His Word.

Let me remind y'all of this — sermons, books, devotions, meetings, and all of the other "good things" we use to help us on our journeys are all needed. However, none of those will ever replace THE WORD OF GOD and your intimate relationship with Him. To be honest, if you are going to leave anything out, leave out everything else, but keep God's relationship with you and His Word first because without those two things you have nothing.

These two things are the weapons that no devil in hell or on earth, or anywhere else, for that matter, can defeat. Those two weapons will get you through ANYTHING that comes your way. God's Word has the answer to EVERY issue you will ever face. It is not called the Living Word for nothing, I promise you.

You can read the same verse a hundred times and get a hundred different messages from God about it. He will give you exactly what you need at the exact time. Remember Jeremiah 33:3: *"Call to me and I will answer you and tell you great and unsearchable things you do not know."* There you have it. He tells you right there in His Word that He will tell you everything you need to know when you need to know it. All you have to do is search. The only way you can be sure it is coming from Him is either when He tells you in your intimate conversations, or when He tells you from His Word. Either way, you must be in communication with Him to hear these things.

He will use those other avenues as well to confirm things, but the one thing I have really grown to see is that if I feel He is telling me something from any other source than Himself or the Word, I take it to Him for confirmation. It will happen.

Remember, His Word is ALL TRUTH! God is not a man that He should lie, and God does not change his mind. Numbers 23:19: *"God is not human that He should lie, not a human being that He should change His mind."*

Also, we must remember that God's word is what He uses to speak truth to us and guide us. It is NEVER wrong. Psalm 119:105. *"Thy Word is a lamp unto my feet, a light on my path."*

Everything you need to know is right there, but you will never know if you don't spend the time. Think about it this way, would you rather spend your time stressing, worrying, and trying things on your own and failing over and over again, or would you rather take the time to talk to Him and be obedient to what He says the first time, watching it all work out and seeing a blessing? Yeah, I'll take the latter. It won't be completely easy or free of stress, especially in the beginning, but it will be so much easier than doing it on our own and over and over again. I promise you.

All we need to really see is that true *love* is the exact same *love* God gives to us, and we are to do our best to mimic that to others. There is no way we can do that on our own, yet with the Holy Spirit leading us, we can do anything. That is exactly where we need to be in everything, led by the Holy Spirit. When we do this, we can overtake and conquer any Goliath that comes our way. When it feels impossible to *love* and have faith and hope in someone, think about how God does it for us when we mess up and do all we do. If you really look at it that way and do not focus on your feelings, then it's not as tough as you may think.

Chapter Seven

NO MATTER WHAT!

Now that we have completely dissected what the Bible tells us that *love* really is, we come to what I feel is the last and most important part of it all. This part is very important to me, and I will hang on to it for life. I think it is so strategic of God to make this the last point in the verse, because it literally ties it all up from everything we have learned since the beginning of the verse.

The very last characteristic of *love* is this: "*Love endures through EVERY circumstance.*"

This one sentence is so powerful, I am crying as I write this. I remember a time when reading this would not mean very much, and most likely would even piss me off, yet who would have ever — and I mean *ever* — think I would be here reading that same sentence now and having to stop writing because I couldn't see past all of my tears?

What changed? you may be asking yourself.

The one thing that finally changed for me was knowing this exact type of *love* and feeling it for myself . . . God's *love* and the *love* He has for me is simply unexplainable. Once you finally begin to trust Him, and allow yourself to feel His *love* for you, it is a feeling that you will never want to give up. You will be dumbfounded by how much He loves you, even with all of the crap you have done and will continue to do.

Through it all, He was always there. His *love* never ever diminished because of what we did. He actually loved us so much, He sent his only son to die for you and me as I have mentioned before. That alone is crazy. My babies are everything to me, and for me to *love* someone so much I would sacrifice one of my kids ... NEVER! Yet that is EXACTLY what He did for you and me. WOW! And this is exactly why I cry. He *loves* each of us this much, and He is simply waiting for us to choose Him.

Think about that for a second. If He loves us this much then why, and I mean why, wouldn't He give us and do for us all the things that will be best for us? That's exactly what He wants to do for us, but He cannot if we do not allow Him to. He will never just do it. He is waiting, lovingly and patiently, for us to call upon Him. I picture Him standing there at the starting line, just ready to take off for us and win this thing. But He will not go until we give Him the signal.

Once we do, He is off and running fast on His way to win this thing with flying colors, ready to smoke everyone in His path. Yet here we come, getting in the way and picking things up and trying to do it again on our own. When we do this, He stops and lets us. Ugh, you see how frustrating it is when we look at it that way. He is winning by far in this race, and everyone is cheering, and now He must stop. Everyone else not only catches up but passes Him, because here we are getting involved yet again. Can you imagine if I saw this play out on TV?

I'd be screaming at this person, *"SIT DOWN AND MOVE OUT OF THE FRICKIN' WAY SO HE CAN WIN THIS THING! O.M.G. WHAT IS YOUR PROBLEM, FOOL?!!!!!"*

It's crazy when you see it this way, right? God shows me things in crazy ways, but He will do whatever it takes to get my attention. This is an example of how much He *loves* us and desires to be with us. Chew on that one for a bit. Who do you know that will *love* you so much that they will sacrifice His own child and do all these things just because they want to spend time with YOU and *love* you in ways you can never imagine? It cannot be done, no matter how hard we try. Only God can love this way, and He wants to *love* each of us this way. All we have to do is let Him.

This is just so powerful to me. *"Endures through every circumstance."* When you read this, you may think it kind of sounds like not giving up, and we already went over that.

That is exactly what I thought, too, but it's not that at all. Not giving up means you keep going no matter how you may feel. You just keep pushing through, no matter what it takes. Enduring through every circumstance means so much more. It means that *Love* endures through every circumstance.

Let's first look at the actual meaning of the word circumstance. Circumstance is defined as a fact or condition connected with or relevant to an event or action. Pretty much anything. Any action or event ever done or about to be done. No matter what it is, *love* will endure through it all. Meaning, it's not just quitting, it is remaining in *love* no matter what the circumstance may be.

This one is crazy tough. This type of *love* can ONLY be accomplished with God. Think about this . . . no matter what is done to you, what you may go through or what someone may put you through, intentionally or not, *love* will always remain. Pretty impossible in our eyes, right? So someone can hurt you in the worst way or harm your child, or someone you *love*, and yet we must still *love* them regardless? Yep, that is it. That is the meaning.

True *love*, the *love* that God loves with, the only type of *love*, loves no matter what. This is exactly how He loves each and every one of us. No matter how much we may hate Him or not choose Him or sin and spit in His face, He still dearly loves us and desires for us to come to Him. Look at the Israelites. O.M.G. God did everything for them, and yet the second they could, they would turn on Him and betray Him in some way.

The Bible even tells us it broke His heart every single time, and even though He got to the point of giving them dire consequences, He still loved them so much that, when they would come crying to Him and want Him to help them, He always did, even knowing they would repeatedly betray and hurt Him. Can you imagine that? That is a *love* that we will never understand until we see Him face to face.

This breaks my heart, because this is exactly what we do to Him when we sin and turn away from Him. We are the Israelites of the present. And when I think about that, it just kills me to know that He loves me, and I break His heart every time I try to do things my own way.

There is no possibility that we can even begin to *love* others in this same exact way. However, we can try, which is all He asks of us. We will be able to do it in such a greater capacity than we even know if we do it with Him at the forefront. Let Him lead. It actually becomes easier and easier, trust me. I now can *love* people who have hurt me and my children in horrendous ways, and the only way I am able to do this is because the Holy Spirit lives within me and guides me.

I have learned this is the God who loves me so much, He is not asking me to *love* others this way just for their benefit. He asks this of me and us for our benefit, as well. When we harbor ill feelings and display a lack of forgiveness, it only kills us inside. But when we *love* freely, it is healing to our souls.

It may seem impossible now, but I promise you, the Word doesn't lie. The Word states many times that God is the God of impossibilities.

Mark 10:27: *Jesus looked at them and said, "With man this is impossible, but not with God; all things are possible with God."* The straight Power and *Love* in this verse alone is everything. Think about it. ALL THINGS — not some, not a few, not only the easy things — ALL things are possible with God.

Think about every situation you have written off. The marriage from hell, the unsaved friend or family member, the impossible healing, the impossible dream or circumstance. Now turn it all around and think about this . . . God can make it all possible. Every single thing. If you put Him at the center of your life and walk together with Him, He can do anything and wants to do it for you. Now this may hit some people a bit differently, because you may be reading this and saying to yourself, *"Well, I wanted God to do this impossible thing, and He did not do it for me."*

This may be true, but we must remember that not everything we may ask Him to do is His will for us or the people we are praying for. This is why we have to stay in close relationship with Him so that we know what His will is and when we are this close to Him we must trust that His desires will soon be our desires, as well.

When we are that close to God, we will find that the things that once mattered most to us tend to not matter as much anymore. Remember when I begged God to do something for me, and I was upset when He didn't, yet later I thanked Him for not listening to me.

There are reasons when God says no and when it happens, I guarantee that it is for the best for us even if we do not see it at that time. We also should be careful when we pray for things for others, because we do not know their relationship with God or His will for them. We have to trust that He does what is best for them, and not just for us.

I remember a time when God called me to go and pray for these two people in the hospital. Two separate occasions, and nothing connected them, although they were within weeks of each other. I prayed for a woman I did not know, yet she was the mom of someone at my children's school, and for another person who meant a great deal to me. The woman had cancer, and the gentleman had a heart attack.

I obeyed God even though it seemed crazy to me. I drove hours to both because they were in ICU at different hospitals. I prayed for them right at their bedsides, and I continued to pray at home. Sadly, both passed away within days of me praying, which made me furious at God at this point.

Yep, I was furious. I mean, how could He tell me to pray in front of their families and they then passed away? After my dramatic meltdown, I began to pray and asked God, why? It was at that moment that He spoke to me in such a loving voice — and I remember this so, so clearly. He said to me, *"Andrea, I asked you to go and pray for them and you did just that. I never told you that they would be healed. What you do not see is that your obedience is what I needed at the time. You may not see it now or even understand, but I see things you do not see and you need to trust me."*

Long story short, the man I prayed for did pass, but his entire family was saved because of my obedience, and many others as well just by that one deed. As for the woman, I have no idea what my obedience caused, but it's okay. God knows, and that is all that matters. We are called to obey. We will be blessed because of it, and so will many others as well, even if we do not see it.

So in all of this, we see that we are completely able to *love* anyone and everyone through every circumstance with the help of The Holy Spirit. In doing so, it will not only bless us and our descendants but others as well. Nothing is impossible for God, and He would never ask us to do anything that He does not equip us to do. We may not feel in our flesh that we are capable of doing great and mighty things, but believe it is possible if He has called you to it. He will equip you for it in every possible way. All we need to do is trust Him and take that leap of faith. He will do the rest. Just look at David and Goliath.

Chapter Eight

THE WRAP-UP OF TRUTH

We have now examined nearly every aspect of the word *love* and every characteristic that makes up the word. We know exactly what God expects of us, and we now know exactly how much He loves us. We also know that we are quite capable of loving others this exact way with the leading of The Holy Spirit. What blows my mind is that after reading and studying all of this, *love* is nothing like I thought it was.

We all casually use the word *love*, which is sad. We throw the word around, using it to get what we want or using it to describe our feelings for food or material things. It's nothing at all to what God says about it. The Bible tells us in 1 Corinthians 13:13 that out of everything, the greatest thing is *love*. Because out of all the commandments and things God asks of us in relation to how we treat others, if we *love* them the way *love* is meant in the Word, then all of the other commandments fall right in line along with it.

If you *love* people, you surely cannot hurt them in any way. We are to really *love* others, which will take care of the rest. Pretty crazy when you look at it that way, right? The one thing that blows my mind is the realization that *love* is the one thing everyone — yes, I do mean EVERYONE — desires. Oh, you can tell yourself you don't or that you don't need anybody or that *love* doesn't matter to you. All of those statements are lies.

If you really examine yourself and your heart, you will find that most of the time those types of feelings and words are just spoken from a wounded and broken heart. We all want nothing more than to be loved just as we are, and it may be that at one time or another, or maybe even numerous times in many cases as is mine, people have told us they loved us. But they have broken our hearts and crushed our spirits in such a way that the walls of Jericho have nothing on the walls we've built around what's left of our hearts in order to protect them.

I completely understand this concept because I have lived there most of my life. However, not once in God's Word will you find where it says, *"Once you are hurt, build walls and never love again."* You will find, however, that it does say in Proverbs 4:23, *"Above all else, guard your heart, for everything you do flows from it."*

This is awesome to me because it tells me that God knows what's best. And if we take everything to Him first, as I stated previously, then He will surely tell us if someone is right for us or not, whether it be a romantic relationship or a friendship. If He tells us no, then we know the outcome will not end well if we disobey and then it will all be on us.

God will give us wisdom on everything and anything we ask Him, but we have to be in that intimate relationship with Him and the more you communicate with Him, the closer you will be, just like any relationship, only the best part of this relationship is that He will always tell you the truth and do what is best for you.

As I said before, *love* is everything and everyone desires it. God made us this way and He is the one who put that desire in our hearts. We all crave true *love* whether it be in a romantic relationship, in a family dynamic, or in a friendship. Whichever way, it might be that the reality will always be the same, we all want to be loved with the true *love* God intended for us and just as we are.

I am about to be so raw and transparent here, it goes against

EVERYTHING in my own flesh. But if it can help just one single person, then what the heck! By all means, I will spill my guts out on the floor for all to see. Do with them as you please, because it will all be worth it to me if it helps just that one person, who hurts in the way I did.

You see, *love* is something that I have craved all my life. I remember being young and always being the "mean kid" — the one everyone was afraid of. I never understood why because this was not how I wanted to be seen at first. I wanted so much to be loved and accepted, yet it never seemed to end up that way. My outside never matched what I felt inside. Looking back, I now know that the enemy knows one's deepest desire as well and He will definitely use it against you every chance he gets . . . that relentless fool!

Also, the enemy always gets us as children first. It is then that he thinks he can ruin us for the rest of our lives . . . These are all the lies that he wants us to believe. Anyhow, as I got older, the one thing that I never lacked was — O.M.G., here we go — attention from guys. Oh, I had them everywhere. If one didn't work, there were always more and everywhere I turned. As I got older, it only became worse. With all of that said, I always wound up with the most toxic ones possible. Every one I chose was worse than the one before.

No matter how much I tried to choose differently on the outside, the inside was always the same. Toxic, abusive, and everything that comes with it. Of course, I was now at a place in which I never felt good enough, and I also began to believe all the lies the devil continued to throw at me. If there was a good guy in the bunch, I wanted nothing to do with him even if I said I wanted a good guy. It was as if I was a magnet for these abusive types of men, and I never understood why until now. It carried well into my marriages; yes, you read that correctly. Marriages. No matter how much I thought it wouldn't.

I was even a Christian, who followed God in my adult life, yet none of it changed. I felt completely worthless, rejected, and hopeless. Without getting into too much detail, after my most recent divorce, I wanted to end my life. So much so that I prayed for God to kill me and my son as we were driving so that He could take us both quickly and we would not have to feel any more pain.

Was I a believer? Yes.

Was I going to church and reading and doing all of the "things" that Christians do? For the most part, yes.

Was I praying? Yes. And yet, I still felt this way. This was so traumatic to me, I no longer wanted to live. Long story shortened, God brought me through all of that pain and delivered me to where I am today.

I arrived here with my youngest, and we knew no one. No family or friends here, but I heard God's answer when I asked Him where He wanted me to go. I was close to God then, but just not as close as I am now. You will see what I mean in a bit.

At first, it felt like a whole different ballgame. God began to move. Oh, it all felt like hell at first. A hell like I can't even begin to explain to you. After being married for so many years, as well as experiencing the trauma it caused me and my kids, this felt so foreign to me. And yet God was with me every step of the way, and even though I thought I knew no one here, God brought a few angels my way. Who would have thought?

I had been here for about two years when God really started to move and shake me. He blessed me in so many ways, I lost count. He opened so many doors for me, and the blessings kept pouring in even through my pain. He still had so much more for me. He needed to isolate me in order to start the refining process. He literally stripped me of everything I held close to my heart. My kids, my family, and my angel. Finally, I was left with just me.

Being alone frightened me, especially because what I desired was to be loved. The details are beyond belief and so numerous, I began to write another book. For now, we will just stick to the subject at hand. *Love.* God told me Himself that His intent on getting me here and all alone was to teach me what true *love* really was. He told me that what I knew of *love* and what I desired was not at all what I thought. He told me He would teach me the true meaning of *love* by showing me how much He loves me.

He said He would do this by sending me many people who needed *love*, too. But I could not help them until I understood *love* and accepted it fully myself. It's one thing to understand it on paper, but to see yourself in the way God sees you, especially when it goes against everything you see and believe about yourself, is impossible without God.

There is no way we could ever *love* anyone truly without first loving ourselves and allowing God to *love* us. I am literally sobbing as I write this, because this is not something that I learned in the past. I am learning as I write this book. He has been teaching me all of this in the present, and it simply blows my mind.

Once God revealed all of this to me, I remember changing my mind set and deciding to just give in and let Him do whatever He needed to do. Why? you might ask. Because I was tired of this rollercoaster life, full of disappointment and heartache. I figured things couldn't get much worse than what I'd already endured.

It was at this point one day, I was crying and wondering, *Will I ever find the love I desire, and does it even exist?* I felt certain I would be alone forever because I refused to allow anyone to hurt me again. Everyone who'd ever said they loved me had hurt me in such awful ways.

I finally concluded that *love* was not part of my destiny, and I was alright with that reality because I didn't intend to allow anyone to hurt me ever again. There is the lie I mentioned earlier. If I believe it and go with it, then I am living in sin. God calls us to *love* everyone, right? Exactly where the enemy wants me to be . . .

God loves me enough not to leave me alone in my mess. I am

one sheep He came for and left the ninety-nine . . . so are you! One day as I prayed and cried out, God gave me a vision so clear it just blew my mind. I still remember it like it happened five minutes ago.

I had a vision of me running like crazy, back and forth, over and over again. I couldn't see clearly, but as I became more and more curious, the vision became more and more clear. I saw myself darting from person to person and thing to thing. When I stopped focusing on me, I saw God in the background, His arms stretched out, waiting so lovingly and patiently, but what I noticed more than anything was His face. I saw His face so clearly, and the pain I saw in His expression was heartbreaking.

He simply stood there, waiting, and He never once lowered His arms or turned away. Then I went to Him, and He hugged me tightly. In that moment, I saw His face change. It was so full of *love* and joy. If I'd never seen this vision, I would have never known that type of *love*.

I looked again, and I saw myself begin to squirm in His arms, as if trying hard to escape His embrace. And that was exactly what I was trying to do. As soon as I got free of His arms, His poor face became so filled with sadness once again that His pain seemed much worse. The vision was so real. So much so that my heart felt the pain. I asked God what the vision meant, and why it kept happening.

It was then that He revealed the meaning to me. I wanted to die. He told me that that was exactly how our relationship had unfolded during my entire life. He then asked me a question.

One thing I've learned in my journey with God is that He never just flat out tells me things. He always asks questions and makes me answer them even though He already knows the answers. As I type this, He is telling me that it has always been that way with Him. In the Bible He would always ask someone what it was they wanted from Him before He healed them — even when it was completely obvious.

He then clearly and in the most loving way — if you could

just hear Him speak, the *love* you feel is like no other — asked, *"Andrea, who was there every time you were hurt?"*

I then answered, *"You."*

"Who always provided for you when you needed anything?"

"You."

"Who was there every time you called no matter where, when or what time?"

"You."

"And who will never leave you or forsake you?"

With tears running down my face, just as they are now, I answered Him one last time. *"You."*

He then said to me, *"Andrea, yes, it was me, and it will always be me, because I love you more than anyone ever could. I sat for years and watched you run to everything and everyone but me. I never forced myself on you or made you come to me. I simply waited for you to choose me, yet every time someone or something hurt you, you came running back to me. I was so full of joy until you found something else and ran away from me again.*

"I knew that it would always end up the same as before, if not worse, but I had to let you figure this out for yourself. Even though it hurt me tremendously to watch you repeatedly get hurt, it was not time for me to intervene. It was not until now. You have finally come to the end of yourself and to the place where you are finally tired enough to give it all to me and let me take over. It is what I have always wanted for you.

"I wanted to love you, take care of you, and to give you only the best, but you had to be at the point where you really wanted me to. You are now there, and we are going to do this together. Believe me, I know exactly what you need, and I know the exact desires of your beautiful little heart, because I made it. And I am the one who put it all there. I want you to have all of those things you truly desire, and so much more. You know now that you've put me first and surrendered everything to me. I have that love for you that you have been desiring, and I am the only one who can give you that kind of love.

"I understand that you desire to be in a kingdom marriage with the one man I have chosen for you. That is nothing for me to do for you, even

though you may think it is impossible. I already know who he is, but I could not get Him to you until you realized that your one true love was me the whole time.

"*Now that you and I are so close, I am certain that when I send your husband to you, you will not put him above me now because you and I have a relationship that is very strong. However, you do need to keep it that way. I will help you stay focused, but you know how the enemy works, so you need to stay close to me now more than ever, because you are now in my will and purpose for you and the enemy will never leave you alone. Do not worry. Remember my Word. We win and no weapon that is formed against you will ever prosper.*"

When I tell you I was bawling like a baby just as I am now, you could not even imagine my condition. It took days for me to process this whole scene. I had so many emotions going through me, I had no idea what to do. After I composed myself and thanked God for not leaving me in my mess, I truly repented for so many things and just let Him *love* me the way I'd needed Him to all along. It was a struggle, and it will always be work on this side of heaven, but I know now that I am finally on the right path with God and that He is all I need.

At that moment God revealed to me His plan for me to write not only this book but so many others, as well. I was not prepared for this, and I have never done anything like this, but I do know to obey when God tells me something. That being said, here we are. We are all on this journey together and I am no different than anyone else.

God can and will use everyone's unique talents to reach others. That is all He asks of us. He will take care of everything as long as we put Him first. Remember, He will never force you to do anything, but He will *love* you enough to keep trying.

Please don't be as stubborn as I was. I could have saved myself so much pain and heartache — my kids, as well — if I had simply given Him control far sooner. He is, after all, the one who loves me most of all.

I know how hard this may seem to you, and I know how hard

it may be to forgive and to relinquish control, but I promise you — I PROMISE YOU — that once you do this, you will wish you had done it sooner. It is so amazing to embrace such an intimate relationship with God that you would be willing to suffer all over again just to experience this relationship.

Remember, He is there. His arms are open as He waits for you. The decision is yours. Yes, true *Love* does exist, but only with Him and through Him.

CONCLUSION

I am sure your definition of *love* has changed since you first began to read this book. I know mine is now completely different. It is all good, though. Now you are in a place to start to live the life God has called you to live. All God asks of us is that we *love* one another. And yet, there is no way we can do that if we don't fully understand the meaning of the word, and if we don't allow God to *love* us - without His *love*, we can't truly *love* ourselves. We must *love* ourselves first to really *love* anyone else.

Lastly, we will never find *love* in any man, woman, job, friend, family member or anything else until we realize that the only true *love* we will ever find and the one we desperately long for is with God and God alone. He has been there waiting, hoping and wanting to give it to us this whole time. All we need to do is run to Him and never let go, because I assure you, He won't. He wants nothing but to give us the best and all we desire in Him but until we put Him first, He can't.

Why tie His hands any longer? Why prevent Him from winning that race for you? Move out of the way and allow Him to do what only He can do. He will not only win this thing for you in such a mind-blowing way, He will do the impossible in every aspect of your life. Simply ask Him. Let go of you, give it to Him and just Believe!

ABOUT THE AUTHOR

Andrea Martinez has enjoyed writing as far back as she can remember. A wife, mother of three, California native, and successful business owner, everything she writes is from her own life experiences and lessons learned.

Already well into writing her second book, she's eager to share all of her stories with the world. *I Want the Truth* is her debut release, and she gives all of the glory to God.

www.ingramcontent.com/pod-product-compliance
Lightning Source LLC
Chambersburg PA
CBHW030242010526
44107CB00030B/1303/J